The Natural
between acid and alkaline
Balance

OF ACID, ALKALINE AND pH

Do you sometimes feel really "sour" – even "acid"? Or do you feel really worn out? The reason for this may be an imbalance between acid and alkaline in your body. Acid always contains free, positively charged water particles H^+. An alkali consists mainly of negatively charged particles derived from water, containing hydrogen and oxygen: OH^-. The level of acid and alkaline is measured in pH. If this figure is 7, the positively and negatively charged particles are balanced, that is to say, neutral. The alkaline level rises from 7 to 14, and the acid level rises as the pH falls from 7 to 0.

THE BODY: FROM ACID TO ALKALINE

The pH values in our bodies differ from organ to organ. This allows different types of chemical reactions in different parts of the body, each of which occurs only at a specific pH level. In the stomach, where hydrochloric acid is produced, the pH value is very acid. The gall bladder and pancreas also produce acids. Alkaline digestive juices are produced solely in the saliva and in the duodenum. The pH value can vary tremendously throughout our tissues, but it must remain more or less stable at 7.4 in the blood, so slightly alkaline, as otherwise our metabolism would break down. Our body has a buffer system to ensure it stays that way. No matter how well or badly we eat, the main way it works is by constantly changing the amount of acid and alkali discharged by the kidneys into the urine.

IF THE BALANCE IS WRONG

In a healthy body, acid and alkaline are well balanced. However, stress, unhealthy eating, and rushing around can have such an effect on this balance that we start to feel unwell. A modern lifestyle tends to increase the production of acid in the body: fast food, foods with a high protein content, such as meat, cheese, fish, sweets, alcohol, coffee, and tobacco, all produce large amounts of acid. We rush around all day, rarely breathe properly or perspire enough, and do not eat enough alkaline-forming foods.

DO I HAVE TOO MUCH ACID?

Because our bodies have such good buffers, we never really become "acid", and without them we would, soon be ready for a hospital bed somewhere. However, latent over-acidity can become a chronic condition and, in time, put our bodies under pressure.

Excessive acid can accumulate in the tissue, where it makes its presence known. The circulation diminishes, and tissue becomes slack. The body itself soon shows the symptoms of over-acidity: frequent heartburn, gastritis, exhaustion, backache, a "spongy" feel to the skin, brittle hair and finger nails are all typical signs.

HOW TO FIND OUT FOR YOURSELF

The pH content of urine changes through the course of a day. It is affected by the amount of sleep we get, and by eating and drinking. The level should be between 5 and 8. Urine is generally more acid in the morning and evening, and more alkaline at midday and in the afternoon. To get an idea of your internal "chemistry", you should measure the acidity in your urine before and after every meal and before you go to bed. Your local chemist will sell you the test strips. The strips change colour at a pH level of between 5 and 8 on contact with urine. If the figures are outside this range, follow our "Basic Week", and measure again afterward. The best proof, however, is how you feel after changing to an alkaline-forming diet. As your symptoms subside, the basic principles of the eating plan will become more a way of life than a diet and should ideally be adopted for life.

Living the
What works — and how?
alkaline way

WHAT WORKS – AND HOW?

Depending on its composition, all the food we eat produces a certain amount of acid or alkaline in our bodies. Protein is highly acid-forming, carbohydrate alkaline-forming, and fats are neutral. Minerals can be positively or negatively charged. The digestive system also contributes to the end result, and that is why it is not easy to determine the acid- or alkaline-forming potential of a particular food. However, the tables on pages 6 and 7 can be used as a rough guide.

ACID-FORMING FOODS AND DRINKS

A lot of foods and drinks that "set you up" and get you going will cause your body's pH level to drop. Alcohol, coffee, cola, and tea that has not been left to brew properly all cause excess acid. The same applies to fruit teas, and those carbonated drinks that contain phosphoric acid. Chocolate, sugar, confectionery, cakes, biscuits, and white flour are also acid-forming. The last highly acid-forming group of foods consists of meat, sausages, fish, seafood, cheese, and egg white. This means that a vegetarian diet is more likely to be alkaline-promoting than a meat-eating one.

THE NEUTRALS

These are usually slightly acid- or alkaline-forming. Our bodies need the neutrals because they contain vital nutrients. Neutral foods include cultured milk products and milk. Butter, clarified butter, and cold-pressed oils with added vitamin E and beta-carotene provide adequate calories. Amaranth, spelt, millet, quinoa, and buckwheat are all full of protein and vitamin B, and an ideal substitute for the more common types of grain and acid-forming rice.

ALKALINE FOODS

With just a few exceptions, fruit, potatoes, and vegetables are highly alkaline. Even if they taste acidic, such as citrus fruits, they have an alkaline effect. This is also true of vegetables that contain lactic acid, such as sauerkraut. There are vast differences between the different types of pulses: although haricot beans are alkaline-forming, all other dried pulses are acid-forming. Opinions differ with regard to nuts and seeds, but almonds, pumpkin, and sunflower seeds are alkaline-forming. And the fresher they are, the better.

BY THE WAY: Sprouted seeds are always alkaline, and therefore very healthy. Furthermore, fresh seed and bean sprouts are full of vitamins, minerals, and bioactive substances.

WHAT SHOULD I DRINK?

It's important to make sure you drink
enough, as this is beneficial for the kidneys
and helps to flush away acids. Ideally, you
should drink at least 2 litres (3½ pints) per
day. Still mineral water is good, as are mild
herbal teas. Special alkaline-forming teas
are sold in health food stores. Black tea,
provided it is left to brew for at least four
minutes, and malt coffee are also good
choices. Natural fruit and vegetable juices
are alkaline-forming, but almost count as a
snack, and are best diluted with water. As
far as milk products are concerned, the ideal
choice is whey or buttermilk. Fermented
wheat liquid (page 15), diluted 1:1 with still
water, is a wonderful health drink. And if
you don't want to go completely teetotal,
dry wine and beer are fine – in moderation!

AND WHAT ABOUT SNACKS?

Constantly adding undigested food to the
semi-digested food already in our stomach
causes heartburn and over-acidity. It is
therefore better to stick to three meals a
day, with perhaps a little fruit in between
if you are really hungry. Muesli and salads
are ideal cold meals, whereas the popular
sandwich can be highly acid-forming.
Instead, opt for some Spelt and Potato
Bread with a vegetarian spread (pages
16–17).

Foods
acid- or alkaline-forming

Several factors determine whether a food is acid- or alkaline-forming: mineral content, your metabolic system, and its impact on the digestive organs. The following is therefore intended only as a guideline.

IMPORTANT: The food you eat should be 80 per cent alkaline-forming and 20 per cent acid-forming. Eat neutral foods in moderation.

BY THE WAY: Just because something tastes acid, doesn't mean it is. Citrus fruit, kiwi, and pineapple are, like most fruits, highly alkaline-forming. Vegetables that contain lactic acid, such as sauerkraut, capers, pickled gherkins, and olives, are alkaline-forming even though they taste acidic.

RECOMMENDATION: Use organic produce wherever possible. If you wish to avoid genetically modified (GM) foods, read any labels with care and select certified organic produce, as this is not produced from GM ingredients.

ALKALINE-FORMING

Potatoes
Vegetables
Fresh fruit
Dried fruit
Honey
Fruit syrups
Maple syrup
Cane sugar
Sprouts & seeds
Herbs and spices (cinnamon, bay leaf, vanilla, marjoram, dill, mustard, cumin)
Sauerkraut
Capers
Olives
Yeast
Soy sauce
Herbal teas
Still water
Fermented wheat liquid

NEUTRAL – SLIGHTLY ALKALINE-FORMING	NEUTRAL – SLIGHTLY ACID-FORMING	ACID-FORMING
Fresh milk	Spelt	Meat and sausages
Whey	Wholemeal crispbread	Fish
Buttermilk	Sour dough bread	Seafood
Yoghurt	Haricot beans	Egg white
Fresh cream	Brown rice	Cheese
Soy milk	Sesame seeds	Quark
Tofu	Cashew nuts	White flour
Millet	Pistachios	Light-coloured breads
Buckwheat	Almonds	Pasta
Amaranth	Hazelnuts	White rice
Quinoa	Linseed	Corn
Potato flour	Fromage frais	Pulses (apart from haricot beans)
Arrowroot	Cottage cheese	Sugar
Egg yolk	Sour milk products	Chocolate
Butter	Beer	Confectionery
Cold-pressed oils	Dry wine	Peanuts
Vinegar	Black tea (brewed for at least four minutes)	Walnuts
Sunflower seeds		Brussels sprouts
Pumpkin seeds		Artichokes
		Carbonated drinks
		Mallow tea
		Alcohol
		Coffee
		Black tea (brewed for less than one minute)

The Basic
Eating and drinking the alkaline way!
Week

CHANGE THE HABITS OF A LIFETIME!

Do you sometimes feel like escaping to a desert island? Well, try this basic eating plan for a week instead, and see if you still feel the same way at the end of it. If you follow the plan, excess acid will be eliminated from your body and you will soon start to feel fit and relaxed. It could be the beginning of a new, healthier way of life – a life lived the alkaline way. In time, you should gradually re-introduce dairy products and normal grains to your diet. If you decide to follow this plan for the long term, you should also take calcium supplements.

THE WEEK

The weekend before you start to follow this plan, bake some Spelt and Potato Bread, make some Potato Cheese and Fruit Marrow, and prepare some vegetable stock. Buy the ingredients for the Ginger and Nettle tea, a mountain of fruit, and two bottles of fermented wheat drink (page 15). Drink 200ml (7fl oz) fermented wheat drink, at least 1 litre (1 3/4 pints) of mineral water, and as much vegetable stock as you like every day. If you prefer, drink the water hot; you will be amazed at how pleasant it is. You could also start (on the Sunday) with a fruit day to detox your system: eat as much raw fruit and vegetables as you like. Make sure you leave at least two hours between meals. There are three main meals a day and two "extras", which you can either eat at mealtimes or as snacks in between – making sure you leave the required gaps between meals. Incidentally, to begin with, you may well experience headaches and weariness, and generally feel "down". That is only to be expected; you will invariably feel a little worse before you start to feel better. Hold out – things will soon change. And last, but not least: if you find you are still hungry after a meal, eat twice the amount!

* Helpful hint: Freeze the bread in portions.

EATING PLAN FOR THE WEEK

Monday

* 1 slice of Spelt and Potato Bread with Potato and Basil Cheese and butter with Cold mixed Fruit Purée * Baked Curried Rösti * Stuffed Tomatoes with 2 slices of Spelt and Potato Bread * Berry and Buttermilk Mix

Tuesday

* Muesli Mix with Spelt and Millet * Haricot Bean Stew
* Rocket and Wild Rice Salad with 1 slice of Spelt and Potato Bread
* Pumpkin Salsa Verde with raw or steamed vegetables

Wednesday

* 2 slices of Spelt and Potato Bread with Potato and Basil Cheese and butter, Fruit Marrow or honey * Potato and Tomato Cocktail, followed by Plum Dumplings * Marinaded grilled Fennel with boiled new potatoes * Butterhead and Quinoa Salad * Milk Mix with Pears and Cinnamon

Thursday

* Amaranth Muesli * Green Asparagus Mousse with boiled new potatoes
* Provençal Salad with 2 slices of Spelt and Potato Bread
* Cream of Basil Soup

Friday

* Sprouted Muesli * Potato Gratin * Dandelion Salad with Kidney beans and 1 slice of Spelt and Potato Bread * Chocolate Pudding * 1 slice of Spelt and Potato Bread with Potato and Basil Cheese or Honeyed Fruit

Saturday

* 1–2 slices of Spelt and Potato Bread with Honeyed Fruits, 1 Berry and Buttermilk mix * Vegetable Tempura with Tomato Sauce * Green Pasta Salad with Potato and Tomato Cocktail * Blackcurrant Sorbet * Pepper Carpaccio

Sunday

* Spelt and Potato Bread with Honeyed Fruits, Potato and Basil Cheese
* Beetroot Ragout * Tomato and Asparagus Salad
* Cream of Pumpkin Soup

Fresh

delicious with

Honeyed

citrus fruits

Fruit

Serves 4: • 120ml (4fl oz) runny honey • 1 kiwi • 1 nectarine • 1 tbsp lemon juice •
100g (4oz) wild strawberries or raspberries • 2 tbsp blueberries

Spread 2–3 tablespoons of honey over the bottom of a flat dish. Peel the
kiwi and cut into 5mm (1/4 in) slices. Slice the nectarine and sprinkle with
lemon juice. Pick over the berries, wash if necessary, and pat dry. Spread
the fruit over the honey and cover with the remaining honey. The fruit will
keep for 1 week if stored in an airtight container in the refrigerator.

TOTAL: 123 kcal • 1 g protein • 1 g fat • 32 g carbohydrate

Ginger and Nettle Tea
diuretic, invigorating, and alkaline-forming
with Liquorice

Ingredients for 1 litre (13/4 pints) of tea: • 1 finger-sized piece of ginger root • 1 piece liquorice • Nutmeg • 3 tbsp nettle tea • 1 unwaxed orange • 1 litre (13/4 pints) boiling water

Finely chop the ginger and liquorice and place in a teapot with the nettle and some freshly ground nutmeg. Pour over the boiling water and leave to infuse for 10 minutes. Wash the orange, cut into slices, and place in heat-resistant glasses. Strain the tea onto the orange slices. Drink hot or cold.

TOTAL: 18 kcal • 0g protein • 1 g fat • 4 g carbohydrate

Berry and
with agave juice and vanilla pod
Buttermilk Mix

Serves 2: 100g (31/2 oz) berries (fresh or frozen) • 250 ml (8fl oz) buttermilk • 1 vanilla pod • 1-2 tbsp agave syrup

Sort and wash the berries, then drain. Place in a mixing bowl with the whey. Slit the vanilla pod open. Using a sharp knife, scrape out the seeds and add the pod to the whey. Add the agave syrup and blend all the ingredients well. Pour into glasses and serve with a straw.

PER DRINK: 97 kcal • 1 g protein • 1 g fat • 23 g carbohydrate

Milk Mix with
mild and full of calcium
Pears and Cinnamon

Serves 2: • 1 pear • 250ml (8fl oz) full-fat milk • 1/2 tsp ground cinnamon • 1-2 tsp acacia honey

Wash and peel the pear. Cut into quarters, and remove the core and stalk. Blend with the milk, cinnamon, and honey. Pour into tall glasses and serve with straws.

Per Drink: 203 kcal • 2 g protein • 2 g fat • 17 g carbohydrate

Potato and Tomato
with acid-binding potato juice
Cocktail

Serves 2: • 500gr (1lb 2oz) potatoes or 100ml (31/2 fl oz) potato juice • 1 tbsp cider vinegar • 2 tbsp capers with liquid • 2 basil leaves • 250ml (8fl oz) tomato juice • 1 pinch of herb salt • Black pepper

Wash, peel, and purée the potatoes. Sprinkle the vinegar over the potatoes and leave to stand for 10 minutes before passing through a fine sieve. Wash the basil leaves and pat dry. Finely chop the capers and basil leaves. Combine with the potato, tomato juice, salt, and pepper. Serve immediately in cocktail glasses.

Per Drink: 72 kcal • 3 g protein • 1 g fat • 16 g carbohydrate

Spelt and
with alkaline-forming fermented wheat drink
Potato Bread

Wash the potatoes and cook them in a steamer for 20-30 minutes. Peel them while still hot and push through a potato ricer. Combine the yeast and the spelt flour, and add gradually to the riced potatoes.

The dough should be of a soft, malleable consistency. Thin with a little fermented wheat liquid if the mixture is too stiff. Leave to rise at room temperature for 1 hour, then add the salt, cumin, and half the sunflower seeds. Knead the dough gently. Grease the inside of the loaf tins and sprinkle with 50g (1¾ oz) sunflower seeds. Place the dough in the tins and sprinkle over the remaining sunflower seeds. Place the tins in the bottom of a cold oven, heat to 200°C/400°F, and bake for about 1 hour. Leave to cool in the tins, then remove.

**Ingredients for 2 loaf tins
(each 2-litre/3½ pint capacity):**
500g (1lb 2oz) floury potatoes
500g (1lb 2oz) spelt flour
500g (1lb 2oz) wholemeal spelt flour
2 sachets active dried yeast
Fermented wheat liquid
2 tbsp salt
1 tsp cumin
200g (7oz) sunflower seeds

Fermented wheat liquid

This liquid, high in lactic acid, is made by the addition of water to wholemeal bread. The resulting fermentation produces a highly alkaline liquid with highly beneficial biologically active substances. For example just 100ml (3½ oz) of the drink provides you with half your daily requirement of vitamin B12. If the bottled product is not available, pickled cabbage juice can serve as a substitute.

PER PORTION:

202 kcal

8 g protein

5 g fat

31 g carbohydrate

Potato and
ideal on bread
Basil Cheese

Wash the potatoes and steam in their skins. In the meantime, steep the almonds in boiling water, then rinse in cold water and remove the skins.

Ingredients for one 300ml (10fl oz) jar:
200g (7oz) floury potatoes
50g (1³/₄oz) almonds
4-5 tbsp olive oil or whey
1 bunch of basil
1 clove garlic
1 tsp salt
Black pepper

Wash the basil, shake dry, and tear off the leaves. Peel and crush the garlic. Purée the almonds, olive oil or whey, basil, salt and pepper.

Peel the hot potatoes and blend to a paste with the other ingredients. Add salt and pepper to taste.

The spread will keep for 3-4 days in a screw-top jar in the refrigerator.

Potatoes

In folk medicine, potatoes are regarded as a universal panacea. Although highly alkaline, they are full of protein. Grain protein is an ideal accompaniment, so bread with Potato and Basil Cheese can definitely hold its own against a steak sandwich. To retain their nutrients, potatoes are best steamed in their skins.

TOTAL:

830 kcal

16 g protein

68 g fat

42 g carbohydrate

Cold-Mixed

contains no acid-forming sugar

Fruit Purée

Ingredients for one 300ml (10fl oz) jar: • 100g (3 1/2 oz) ready-to-eat prunes • 100g (3 1/2 oz) raisins • 100g (3 1/2 oz) dried figs • 125ml (4 fl oz) orange juice • Ground cinnamon

Wash the dried fruit in hot water, drain on paper towels and then chop. Place in a bowl, pour over the orange juice, and leave to stand for 1 hour. Purée and season to taste with cinnamon. Stored in the refrigerator in an airtight container, this mixture will keep for up to 2 weeks.

TOTAL: 800 kcal • 9 g protein • 3 g fat • 193 g carbohydrate

Cold-Mixed

alkaline-forming with cane sugar

Jam

Ingredients for one 300ml (10fl oz) jar: • 200g (7oz) redcurrants • 125g (4 1/2 oz) strawberries
• 125g (4 1/2 oz) cane sugar

Pick over and wash the redcurrants and strawberries and leave them to drain. Push the topped and tailed redcurrants through a coarse sieve. Cut any large strawberries into smaller pieces. Beat the redcurrant purée, strawberries, and cane sugar in an electric mixer for 10 minutes until the mixture begins to thicken. Stored in a screw-top jar in a cool place, the jam will keep for 4-6 weeks.

TOTAL: 576 kcal • 3 g protein • 1 g fat • 138 g carbohydrate

Muesli Mix with

a high-quality breakfast

Spelt and Millet

Place the grains and poppy seeds in a saucepan with the water and simmer gently for 1 minute. Cool, then chill until ready to use. Peel the

Serves 2:

3 tbsp coarsely ground fresh spelt

3 tbsp coarsely ground fresh millet

2 tbsp freshly ground poppy seeds

1 cup water

1 small banana

200ml (7fl oz) milk

1 pink grapefruit

1 orange

banana, blend with the milk, and combine with the grain mixture. Divide this mix between two bowls.

Peel the grapefruit and orange with a very sharp knife, removing all the pith. Cut the fruits into finger-thick slices, and cut each slice into eight. Arrange the fruit pieces on the muesli and serve immediately.

Grains

Cereals contain good quantities of fibre, vitamins, and phytochemicals, but they also contain phytic acid, which may prevent minerals from being absorbed in the digestive tract. Phytic acid loses its efficacy when cooked, baked, or sprouted. Too much bran – a concentrated source of phytic acid – is undesirable, but, as part of a balanced diet, grains are very nutritious.

PER PORTION:

272 kcal

10 g protein

7 g fat

43 g carbohydrate

power

Amaranth
with apple purée and figs
Muesli

Wash and peel the apple. Cut in half and remove the core, then chop into small pieces. Wash the figs and apricots, drain, and chop into small pieces.

Serves 2:
1 large apple
2 dried figs
6 dried apricots
250ml (8fl oz) water
1 cinnamon stick
1-2 tbsp honey
8 tbsp "popped" amaranth

Place in a saucepan with the apple, water, and cinnamon and bring to the boil. Cook gently for about 5 minutes. Stir in the honey. Leave the apple purée to cool and remove the cinnamon stick. Divide the apple purée between two dishes and serve with the "popped" amaranth immediately.

Amaranth

Amaranth is a seed from the Andes and is less acid-forming than European cereals. Its protein is far more valuable to our bodies than cereal protein. Since it contains no gluten, it is not suitable for baking with yeast. Amaranth is available "popped" from wholefood and health stores. It is also available as a grain, which can be ground either in the store or, if you prefer, by you at home. Substitute with bulgar wheat or coarse ground millet if unavailable.

PER PORTION:

282 kcal

5 g protein

3 g fat

65 g carbohydrate

power

Sprouted
low in calories and invigorating
Muesli

Place the seeds in a preserving jar, cover with warm water, and leave to soak for 24 hours. Drain the seeds, rinse, and return to the jar. Fill with water and leave to stand for a short while. Cover the jar with muslin and secure with a rubber band. Place upside down on a dish rack to allow the water to drain away. Leave the seeds to shoot for about 5 days, until the delicate sprouts appear. Water daily. Then wash thoroughly and leave to drain.

Pick over and wash the berries, then drain. Add the berries to the tiny millet shoots. Combine the yoghurt and maple syrup, mixing until smooth and creamy, then pour over the berry-sprout mixture.

Serves 2:
100g (3½ oz) millet seeds (easy sprouting, from health food stores)
1 cup of berries of choice
150ml (5fl oz) live yoghurt
1-2 tbsp maple syrup

Seed and bean sprouts

Sprouting reduces the amount of fat and phytic acid and increases the vitamin and mineral content. Sprouted seeds are less acid-forming and perfectly digestible raw. Wash the sprouts thoroughly in a sieve before eating. You can also stir-fry them or blanch them in boiling water.

PER PORTION:

193 kcal

6 g protein

4 g fat

34 g carbohydrates

power

Rocket and Wild Rice Salad

for an evening meal, snack or packed lunch

Peel and finely chop the ginger and onion. Pare the peel from the lime. Squeeze the lime. Mix the lime juice with a drop of honey, pepper, and the green peppercorns. Marinate the onion and ginger in it overnight.

Place the wild rice in a saucepan with the water, salt, the cumin and lime peel and bring to the boil. Simmer on a low heat for 45 minutes. Leave to cool, then remove the peel.

Wash the rocket, cut into 3-4cm (11/4–13/4in) pieces and slice the radishes. Combine all the ingredients. Stir together the ginger marinade and the oil, season to taste with salt and pepper, and pour over the salad. Arrange the salad on plates and serve.

Serves 2:

1 piece of ginger root
1 red onion
1 lime
Honey
Pepper
1 tsp green peppercorns
100g (31/2 oz) wild rice
200ml (7fl oz) salt
1/2 tsp cumin
1 bunch of rocket
1 bunch of radishes
3-4 tbsp rapeseed oil

PER PORTION: 350 kcal • 9 g protein • 17 g fat • 44 g carbohydrate

Butterhead
with mushrooms and horseradish
and Quinoa Salad

Sauté the quinoa in 1/2 tbsp oil, then add the vegetable stock, bay leaf, and half the thyme. Simmer gently for 15 minutes and leave to cool.

Serves 2:
150g (5oz) quinoa
1 1/2 tbsp olive oil
150ml (5fl oz) vegetable stock
1 small bay leaf
1/2 tsp thyme
1/2 butterhead lettuce
200g (7oz) mushrooms
1 small onion
1/2 clove garlic
1/4 unwaxed lemon
50ml (2 fl oz) whipping cream
1 tbsp sour cream (20% fat)
1 tsp creamy horseradish
Salt and pepper

Wash and drain the lettuce. Wash or wipe the mushrooms and cut into slices.

Peel and finely chop the onion and garlic. Finely grate the lemon peel and squeeze out the juice.

To make the dressing, whip the cream until stiff. Add the sour cream and lemon juice. Season with the lemon peel, the remaining thyme, the horseradish, salt, and pepper.

Heat the remaining oil in a frying pan and sauté the onion, mushrooms, and garlic. Season with salt and pepper.

Carefully combine the dressing with the cooled quinoa and the salad, and divide between two plates. Arrange the mushrooms on top and serve.

PER PORTION: 528 kcal • 19 g protein • 20 g fat • 66 g carbohydrate

Dandelion Leaf Salad

soothes body and mind

with Kidney Beans

Soak the beans overnight in the water. Next day, add the rosemary and bay leaf to the beans and bring to the boil in the same water. Cook for 1 1/2 hours, then add salt and leave to cool. Peel 1 orange down to the fruit and remove the flesh from between the membranes (make sure you save all the juice). Squeeze the juice from the 1/2 orange, grate a pinch of peel, and set aside.

Wash, peel, and dice the carrots. Heat the oil in a saucepan and sauté the carrots. Season to taste with salt and pepper, add a little orange juice, and simmer gently for another 8 minutes.

Wash the chives and dandelion leaves. Chop the chives, and combine with the dandelion leaves, orange segments, diced carrots and cooked beans. Season well. Beat the mustards and cream with the remaining orange juice and peel. Season with salt and pepper. Serve the marinade with the salad.

Serves 2:

100g (3 1/2oz) red kidney beans (dried)

400ml (14fl oz) cold water

1 sprig rosemary

1 small bay leaf

Salt

1 1/2 unwaxed oranges

100g (3 1/2 oz) carrots

1 tbsp oil

Pepper

1 bunch of chives

125g (4 1/2 oz) dandelion leaves

2 tbsp French mustard

1 tbsp English mustard

60ml (2fl oz) whipping cream

PER PORTION: 384 kcal • 16 g protein • 15 g fat • 46 g carbohydrate

Tomato and

with alkaline-forming mustard powder

Asparagus Salad

Wash the asparagus and mangetout peas. Peel the asparagus and cut into 5cm (2in) pieces. Add some salt and the lemon juice to the water and bring to a boil. Boil the asparagus stalk for 5 minutes, then add the asparagus tips and the mangetout. Cook for another 8 minutes.

Meanwhile, wash the tomatoes and cut into segments. Wash and dry the pimpernel (or parsley). Cut away the stalks, and chop the rest. Pass the egg yolk through a fine sieve and combine with the mustard to make a dressing, using some of the asparagus cooking liquid, add 1 tbsp oil, salt, pepper, and half the pimpernel (or parsley).

Combine the dressing with the tomatoes, mangetout, and asparagus and arrange on plates.

Break the crispbread into small pieces. Heat the remainder of the oil, sauté the crispbread until brown, and sprinkle over the salad. Garnish with the remaining pimpernel (or parsley) and serve immediately.

Serves 2:
250g (9oz) white asparagus
75g (3oz) mangetout peas
Salt
1 tbsp lemon juice
100ml (3½ fl oz) water
2 tomatoes
1 bunch pimpernel *or parsley*
1 hard-boiled egg yolk
1 tsp mustard powder or ready-made mustard
3 tbsp cold-pressed olive oil
Pepper
3-4 thin slices crispbread

PER PORTION: 172 kcal • 5 g protein • 11 g fat • 14 g carbohydrate

Marinaded
in herbes de Provence
Grilled Fennel

Pre-heat the oven to 200°C/400°F. Wash the fennel and cut in half widthwise. Remove the green tops from the fennel and set aside. Place two pieces of aluminium foil, shiny side up, on the worktop and rub with the herb oil. Place two fennel halves, cut side down, on each piece of foil. Firmly seal the foil over the top of the fennel. Bake in the centre of the oven for 35 minutes.

Serves 2:
2 heads of fennel, each approx.
300g (10oz)
1/2 tsp herbes de Provence, in oil
125g (41/2 oz) mushrooms (field or oyster mushrooms or chanterelles)
2 tbsp lemon juice
1 clove garlic
11/2 tbsp cold-pressed olive oil
60ml (2fl oz) dry white wine
Salt
Black pepper

Wash and finely slice the mushrooms and sprinkle with 1 tsp lemon juice. Peel and thinly slice the garlic. Heat 1 tbsp oil and sauté the mushrooms in two batches. Pour over the wine, heat through, and place in a bowl.

Add the remaining oil to the pan and gently braise the garlic. Season well with the remaining lemon juice, salt, and pepper, and combine with the mushrooms. Unwrap the fennel, cut into thin slices, and arrange with the mushrooms and fennel tops. Pour over the marinade and leave to stand for 2-3 hours.

Fennel

Fennel is alkaline-forming and aids the body in breaking down acids. It contains 2-3 per cent essential oils, which stimulate the circulation in the digestive tract and respiratory system, and strengthen the stomach, kidneys, and liver.

Per Portion:

145 kcal

5 g protein

8 g fat

8 g carbohydrate

Pepper
with flaked hazelnuts
Carpaccio

Pre-heat the grill to maximum. Wash the peppers and lay on a baking sheet. Place under the hot grill, turning occasionally, until the skins turn black and start to blister. Remove the peppers from the grill and sprinkle with salt. Cover with a damp tea towel and leave to cool. Remove the skins, saving the juice. Cut the peppers lengthwise into 8-10 pieces. Peel and roughly chop the garlic. Squeeze the lime and mix the juice with the pepper juices and the olive oil. Season well with garlic, salt, pepper, and ground paprika. Combine with the pepper strips and juices and leave to marinate for at least 30 minutes. Wash the parsley and shake it dry. Tear off the leaves and chop roughly. Sprinkle the pepper strips with the parsley and flaked hazelnuts. Serve with crispbread, new potatoes, or Spelt and Potato Bread (see page 15).

Serves 2:
1 red and 1 yellow pepper (capsicum)
1/2 green pepper (capsicum)
Salt
1 clove garlic
1/2 lime
2 tbsp cold-pressed olive oil
White pepper
Ground paprika, spicy
1/2 bunch flat leaf parsley
20g (3/4 oz) flaked hazelnuts

Peppers (capsicum)

Peppers are not just highly alkaline; their spicy capsaicin stimulates the circulation and digestion, beta-carotene strengthens the resistance, and bioflavonoids stabilize the blood vessels.

PER PORTION:

185 kcal

4 g protein

15 g fat

10 g carbohydrate

Provençal

extra special with lavender

Vegetable Salad

Serves 2:

250g (9oz) waxy potatoes
150g (5oz) green beans
120ml (4fl oz) water
Salt
1 tbsp herbes de Provence
1 courgette (zucchini)
1 red pepper (capsicum)
1 red onion
1 clove garlic
3 tbsp cold-pressed olive oil
2 tbsp white wine vinegar
Pepper
1 tbsp mustard
1 bunch basil
1 small head radicchio
10 black olives

Wash the vegetables and peel the potatoes. Trim the beans, removing any "strings". In a saucepan, bring the water and 1/2 tsp salt to the boil. Cook the potatoes and beans for 30 minutes. Trim the courgette and cut into small pieces. Halve the pepper, remove the core and seeds, and cut the flesh into small pieces. Peel the onion and garlic and chop finely. Mix together the olive oil, vinegar, pepper, and mustard. Add the vegetable water to the dressing and season to taste.

Peel and slice the potatoes. Pour the dressing over the potatoes and beans. Add the courgette, onion, and garlic, and chill. Wash the basil and shake it dry. Pull the leaves from the stalks and tear roughly. Cut the radicchio into bite-sized pieces. Wash and drain well. Add the basil, olives, and radicchio to the salad. Season well.

PER PORTION: 335 kcal • 10 g protein • 15 g fat • 45 g carbohydrate

Green
vitalizing and highly alkaline
Pasta Salad

Cook the pasta in plenty of salted water until *al dente*. Drain and rinse in cold water. Wash the spinach and the courgettes. Pick over the spinach, remove any hard stalks, and drain. Cut the courgettes into thin slices.

Serves 2:
100g (3½ oz) millet pasta
Salt
125g (4½ oz) baby spinach
150g (5oz) courgettes (zucchini)
½ bunch basil
6 green olives (stoned)
50ml (2fl oz) vegetable stock
1½ tsp lemon juice
Pepper
1 clove garlic
1-2 tbsp grated cheese

Wash the basil, shake dry, and tear off the leaves. Purée in a blender with the olives, stock, and lemon juice. Season with salt and pepper, peel and crush the garlic and add to the dressing.

Carefully combine the pasta and vegetables and pour over the dressing. Arrange the pasta salad on 2 plates, sprinkle with cheese, and serve.

Substitute corn pasta if millet pasta is unavailable.

Spinach

Spinach is one of the most alkaline-rich vegetables. Raw, it contains high levels of vitamins. Large amounts of iron, folic acid, and copper encourage the production of red blood cells, secretin stimulates the pancreas and lutein, an antioxidant, helps protect from eye diseases such as cataracts and macular degeneration. Spinach also contains oxalic acid, which is what causes the "rough" feeling on the teeth.

PER PORTION:

280 kcal

15 g protein

8 g fat

39 g carbohydrate

power

Quinoa Salad with

slightly alkaline evening meal

Cream Vinaigrette

Heat the quinoa in 1 tsp olive oil. Add the lemon juice, water and 1 tsp salt. Bring to the boil, cover with a lid, and simmer gently for 15 minutes. Cool.

Peel and finely grate the beetroot. Crumble the cheese coarsely. Wash the chives and shake dry, then cut into small pieces. Set aside 1/2 tsp. Peel and finely chop the garlic. Wash the cucumber and slice on a mandolin. Lightly combine all these ingredients. Combine the stock, mustard, parsley, remaining chives, pepper, vinegar, remaining oil, and cream to make the dressing. Pour the dressing over the salad just before serving.

Serves 2:
125g (4¹/2 oz) quinoa
4 tsp cold-pressed olive oil
Juice of ¹/2 lemon
400ml (14fl oz) water
Salt
100g (3¹/2 oz) fresh beetroot
80g (scant 3oz) sheep's cheese
1 bunch chives
1 small clove garlic
1 cucumber
60ml (2fl oz) vegetable stock
¹/2 tsp French (mild) mustard
Pepper
1 tbsp mild vinegar
1 tbsp cream

Quinoa

Quinoa is a grain harvested from a cereal-like cultivated plant from South America. Its seeds are small and round, and are slightly alkaline-forming. Like amaranth, quinoa contains more protein than other cereals. It is also high in unsaturated fats, iron, zinc, potassium, magnesium, and vitamin C. Use millet as a substitute if quinoa is not available.

PER PORTION:

409 kcal

18 g protein

16 g fat

48 g carbohydrate

Stuffed

buckwheat filling full of protein and minerals

Tomatoes

Wash the tomatoes, thinly slice the top off to use as a lid, and scoop out the inside with a spoon. Put the tomatoes in a sieve to drain, and season the inside with salt and pepper.

Lightly roast the buckwheat in a non-stick frying pan until warmed through. Wash and thinly slice the spring onions. Peel and finely chop the garlic. Shred the sauerkraut into small pieces. Wash the dill and strip the leaves from the coarse stalks. To make the filling, combine all of the ingredients with salt, pepper, lemon juice, and oil. Season the filling well and divide among the tomatoes. Place the lids on the tomatoes, arrange on plates, and serve.

Serves 2:
6 large tomatoes (approx.1kg/2lb)
Salt
Pepper
120g (4½oz) buckwheat
2-3 spring onions
1 clove garlic
200g (7oz) sauerkraut
1 bunch dill
3-4 tbsp lemon juice
2-3 tbsp rapeseed oil

Alternative Fillings

Use small peppers (capsicum) instead of tomatoes. Try amaranth or quinoa for the filling instead of buckwheat, in which case boil the grains first in 250ml (8fl oz) fermented wheat liquid and leave to cool. Give this dish a more Mediterranean flavour by using basil or herbes de Provence instead of dill.

PER PORTION:

441 kcal

13 g protein

15 g fat

66 g carbohydrate

Spicy
with whey and horseradish
Radish Dip

Serves 2: • 1 bunch radishes • 100ml (3½ fl oz) whey or buttermilk • 50g (2fl oz) whipping cream • 1 tsp creamy horseradish (from a jar) • Salt • Black pepper

Wash the radishes and purée them in a blender, keeping some of the juice to one side. Combine the puréed radishes with the whey. Whip the cream until stiff and combine with the radish purée. Season the dip with the horseradish, salt, and pepper. Depending on the consistency, add a little more of the radish juice (drink the rest) and keep cool.

PER PORTION: 90 kcal • 1 g protein • 8 g fat • 3 g carbohydrate

Pumpkin
with alkaline-forming olives and herbs
Salsa-Verde

Serves 2: • 1 bunch parsley • 1 bunch basil • 50g (scant 2oz) pumpkin seeds • 50g (scant 2oz) green olives (stoned) • 100ml (3½ fl oz) vegetable stock • 2 tbsp olive oil • Salt • Pepper • 1 clove garlic

Wash the herbs, shake them dry and pull off the leaves. Puree the basil and parsley with the pumpkin seeds and olives, and gradually add the stock. Season with oil, salt and pepper. Peel and finely chop the garlic and add to the salsa.

PER PORTION: 259 kcal • 10 g protein • 22 g fat • 9 g carbohydrate

Green
with mascarpone and basil
Asparagus Mousse

Cut the ends off the asparagus, wash it, and peel the lower third. Wash and shake dry the basil and pull the leaves off the stems.

Place the asparagus, basil, and mascarpone in a mixer or blender and purée until smooth and creamy. Combine the purée with salt, pepper, lemon juice, olive oil, and a little of the vegetable or asparagus stock, and season well with salt and pepper.

Serves 2:
100g (3½ oz) green asparagus
½ bunch basil
50g (scant 2oz) mascarpone
Salt
Pepper
1 tbsp lemon juice
1 tsp olive oil
Vegetable or asparagus stock

Dips

These dips are high in protein and fat, and go well with raw or steamed vegetables, pasta and potatoes for a highly satisfying meal. They can easily be prepared in advance and are ideal for a packed lunch.

Mascarpone has a relatively high fat content, but it is less acid-forming than quark. Its high content of valuable lactic acid means the whey is slightly alkaline-forming. You can increase the alkaline effect by adding vegetables to the dip – such as the asparagus used in this recipe. Asparagus is also slightly diuretic, and stimulates the liver and kidneys.

PER PORTION:

145 kcal

3 g protein

13 g fat

5 g carbohydrate

power

Gnocchi

Italian and tasty

with Tomatoes

Wash the potatoes and cook them in a steamer for 20-30 minutes. Peel while hot and push through a potato ricer. Add 1 tsp salt and as much potato flour as is needed until the dough is no longer sticky. Shape into finger-thick rolls on a floured work surface and cut into 3 cm (1¼in) pieces. Flatten each piece with a fork. Bring a generous amount of salted water to the boil. Reduce the heat and simmer portions of gnocchi in the water for 4 minutes. Rinse the gnocchi in cold water and drain. Keep warm on a baking sheet in a very cool oven (80°C/175°F). Peel and quarter the shallots. Sauté in 1 tbsp butter, cover with a lid and simmer with the orange juice for 8 minutes until glazed. Meanwhile, slit the tomato skins and pour boiling water over them. Remove the skins, cut the tomatoes into half and remove the seeds. Cut the flesh into strips. Wash and pick over the sorrel and cut into strips. Add the tomato purée, honey, some paprika, and the remaining butter to the shallots. Heat the tomato strips and sorrel. Season with salt and pepper and serve with the hot gnocchi.

Serves 2:
500g (1lb 2oz) floury potatoes
Salt
3 tbsp flour
2-3 tbsp potato flour
100g (3½ oz) shallots
2 tbsp butter
4 tbsp orange juice
350g (12oz) ripe tomatoes
½ bunch sorrel
1 tbsp tomato puree
Honey
Mild paprika
Pepper

PER PORTION: 322 kcal• 9 g protein • 6 g fat • 58 g carbohydrate

Tomato and Red
with thyme and basil
Pepper Sauce

Wash the tomatoes, remove the stalks, and cut into 8 slices. Halve the red pepper and remove the seeds. Wash and cut lengthwise into 4-6 strips.

Serves 2:
500g (1lb 2oz) ripe beefsteak tomatoes
1 small red pepper (capsicum)
1 onion
1 1/2 tbsp olive oil
1 tbsp tomato purée
1 tsp honey
1/2 sprig thyme
Salt
Black pepper
2 tbsp chopped basil

Peel, halve and chop the onion. Heat the olive oil and cook the onion gently until translucent. Add the tomato and red pepper and stir. Add the tomato purée, honey, thyme, salt, and pepper, and simmer for 30 minutes.

Remove the thyme and purée the sauce or pass through a sieve. Simmer the sauce, uncovered, until thick. Season to taste, and add the basil.

Tomatoes

Tomatoes, like peppers, are highly alkaline-forming, although they do not contain any invigorating fruit acids. They contain high amounts of potassium and magnesium, which support the kidneys and have a diuretic effect. Lycopene, a carotinoid in tomatoes, is associated with a reduced risk of prostate cancer. It also strengthens the immune system. A thickened tomato sauce is an ideal alkaline-forming spread, and delicious on toasted bread.

PER PORTION:

140 kcal

4 g protein

7 g fat

16 g carbohydrate

Cream Sauce
highly aromatic and stylish
with Morels

Serves 2: • 20g (3/4 oz) dried morels • 250ml (8fl oz) water • 1 shallot • 1 tsp butter • 250ml (8fl oz) vegetable stock • 1/2 tsp cornflour • 50ml (scant 2fl oz) whipping cream • Salt • White pepper

Soak the morels in the water for 8 hours, then wipe clean. Strain the soaking water through filter paper. Peel and chop the shallot and cook gently in hot butter until translucent. Add the morels and simmer briefly. Pour in the mushroom water and stock, and cook. Dissolve the cornflour in a little cold water. Whip the cream until thick and add to the cornflour mixture. Pour into the mushroom mixture, heat carefully, and season to taste.

PER PORTION: 116 kcal • 1 g protein • 10 g fat • 5 g carbohydrate

Carrot and
a creamy, alkaline-forming sauce
Almond Sauce

Serves 2: • 200 g (7oz) carrots • 1 onion • 1tbsp butter • 20g (3/4 oz) ground almonds • 2 tbsp tomato purée • 100ml (31/2 fl oz) vegetable stock • Salt • Pepper • Nutmeg • 50ml (scant 2fl oz) cream • Yeast flakes (optional)

Wash, peel and grate the carrots. Peel and dice the onion. Cook both gently in the butter. Add the almonds, tomato purée, and stock. Season with salt, pepper, and freshly ground nutmeg and cook gently for 5 minutes. Purée the vegetables in a blender. Add the cream and season with the yeast flakes (optional).

PER PORTION: 212 kcal• 4 g protein • 17 g fat • 11 g carbohydrate

Haricot
Bean Stew
with plenty of vegetable protein

Chop the tomatoes into small pieces and soak overnight in the water with the beans, the bay leaf, and a few peppercorns.

Serves 2:
3 dried tomatoes
100g (3½oz) dried haricot beans
500ml (18fl oz) water
1 bay leaf
Black peppercorns
1 leek
250g (9oz) potatoes
1 clove garlic
Salt
30g (1oz) pumpkin seeds
1-2 tbsp pumpkin seed oil
1-2 tbsp cider vinegar

Cook the tomatoes and the beans in the soaking water for 30 minutes.

Meanwhile, wash the leek and potatoes. Trim the leek and cut into slices. Peel the potatoes and cut into small dice. Peel and finely chop the garlic.

Add everything to the beans. Season the stew with salt and cook for a further 20 minutes until the potatoes are soft. Brown the pumpkin seeds in a non-stick frying pan. Add to the stew with the pumpkin seed oil and cider vinegar. Season with salt.

Seasonal variations

A delicious summer alternative is to make the stew with fresh tomatoes instead of the dried ones, using 1 pepper and 2 spring onions instead of the leek. In spring, substitute 2-3 new carrots and 2 bunches of sorrel for the leek. You can also use 250g (9oz) chopped leaf spinach and 1 chopped onion.

PER PORTION:
398 kcal
20 g protein
16 g fat
46 g carbohydrate

power

Cream of
with whey and arrowroot
Basil Soup

Serves 2: • 250g (9oz) floury potatoes • 1 onion • 1 clove garlic • 1 tbsp butter • 400ml (14fl oz) whey or buttermilk • Salt • White pepper • 1-2 tsp arrowroot • 1 bunch basil • 2 tbsp sour cream (20% fat content)

Wash the potatoes. Peel and finely chop the potatoes, onion, and garlic. Sauté in the butter until they start to turn brown. Add the whey, season to taste, and cook for 20 minutes. Mix the arrowroot with 2 tbsp water. Add to the potato and whey mixture and bring to the boil. Wash the basil, tear off the leaves, and add. Purée the mixture, and serve garnished with the sour cream.

PER PORTION: 166 kcal • 4 g protein • 4 g fat • 28 g carbohydrate

Cream of
satisfying, mild and highly alkaline-forming
Pumpkin Soup

Serves 2: • 600g (1¼ lb) pumpkin flesh • 1 onion • 1 tbsp olive oil • Salt • Pepper • 200ml (7fl oz) carrot juice • 2 tbsp crème fraîche • Ground ginger • Lemon juice • 20g (¾ oz) currants • 15g (½ oz) roughly chopped pumpkin seeds

Roughly chop the pumpkin flesh. Peel and finely chop the onion. Add both to the oil, season with salt and pepper, and cook over a medium heat for 15 minutes, or until soft. Purée with the carrot juice and crème fraîche. Season with the ginger and lemon juice. Add the currants and pumpkin seeds, heat through, and serve.

PER PORTION: 247 kcal• 6 g protein • 13 g fat• 28 g carbohydrate

Tasty
as a base for sauces, stocks, and stews
Vegetable Stock

Peel and chop the onions. Wipe the mushrooms and cut into slices. Dry-fry the onions and mushrooms in a large pot until they turn dark. Add the fermented wheat liquid and bring to the boil.

Wash, trim and chop the remaining vegetables. Add to the mushrooms with the water, salt, bay leaves, cloves, peppercorns, and herbs and bring to the boil.

Simmer the vegetables over a low heat for 1 hour and leave to cool. Ideally, leave the stock to stand overnight. Pass the liquid through a sieve and season well. The stock will keep for up to 1 week in a sealed container in the refrigerator.

Makes 1 litre (13/4 pints):
2 large onions
100g (31/2 oz) mushrooms
200ml (7fl oz) fermented wheat liquid
500g (1lb) mixed soup vegetables
2-3 ripe or dried tomatoes
1 litre (13/4 pints) water
1 tsp salt
2 bay leaves
2 cloves
1 tsp peppercorns
1 sprig rosemary
2 sprigs thyme

Mushrooms

This stock tastes especially good if you chop the mushrooms, sprinkle them with salt, and leave them for 24 hours. This allows them to ferment; they turn brown and become highly aromatic. Dried mushrooms have a similar effect. You can drink this either hot or cold. Add carrots, pumpkin, or potatoes, cook and purée for an extremely delicious vegetable cream soup.

PER PORTION:
27 kcal
1 g protein
1 g fat
1 g carbohydrate

Vegetable
gentle cooking in a crispy coating
Tempura

Combine the two flours. Mix the egg yolk, the half egg white and about 50g (scant 2oz) of the flour (more if required), iced water, salt, and basil in oil to a smooth batter and place in the refrigerator. Wash and dry the tomatoes. Wipe the mushrooms, and wash them if necessary. Wash and trim the leek and cut into finger-thick slices. Wash again if necessary. Place the vegetables in the refrigerator for 1 hour.

Coat the vegetables in the flour and then dip them in the batter. Melt the coconut in a small saucepan. Cook the vegetables in the coconut until golden brown in colour and drain on paper towels. Sprinkle lime juice over the vegetables and serve with soy sauce.

Serves 2:
40g (1 1/2 oz) amaranth flour
40g (1 1/2 oz) spelt flour
1 egg yolk, 1 egg white
100ml (3 1/2 oz) iced water
Salt
1 tsp basil in oil
100g (3 1/2 oz) cherry tomatoes
150g (5oz) small mushrooms
1 large leek
250g (9oz) creamed coconut
Lime juice
Soy sauce

Deep fried Vegetables
It is important that all the ingredients are cold. Also suitable: broccoli florets, mangetout or sugar-snap peas, strips of pepper (capsicum), slices of courgettes or aubergines, and asparagus. Mashed potatoes made without milk go well with this dish.

PER PORTION:
350 kcal
11 g protein
21 g fat
30 g carbohydrate

Baked Curried
with a carrot and yoghurt dip
Rösti

Wash, trim and thinly slice the spring onions. Peel and finely chop the garlic, setting one-third aside for the dip. Peel and finely grate the ginger.

Serves 2:
2-3 spring onions
2 cloves garlic
1 nut-sized piece of ginger root
600g (1¼ lb) potatoes
Salt
White pepper
1-2 tsp curry powder
2 tbsp chopped cashew nuts
2 tbsp ghee or clarified butter
200g (7oz) carrots
Grated orange peel
150ml (5fl oz) full-fat yoghurt
1 tbsp pumpkin seed oil

Wash, peel and coarsely grate the potatoes, and add the spring onions, garlic, and ginger. Season well with salt, pepper, and curry powder.

Brown the cashew nuts in a large nonstick frying pan with 1 tbsp of the ghee or clarified butter. Place the potato mixture on top, cover with a lid, and fry gently for 10 minutes. Turn, adding the remainder of the ghee or clarified butter, and fry until brown.

Meanwhile, peel and purée the carrots. Combine with the remaining garlic, some grated orange peel, the yoghurt, the oil, salt, and pepper, and season well. Divide the rösti into slices and serve with the carrot yoghurt.

Per Portion: 488 kcal• 11 g protein • 25 g fat • 54 g carbohydrate

Beetroot
served on blinis
Ragout

Mix the flour with the cold water. Stirring constantly, add the hot water, yeast, honey, and 1/2 tsp salt and leave to stand for 1 hour.

Wash and peel the beetroot and cut into thin strips. Peel the onion and cut into semi-circles. Wash, peel and halve the apple. Remove the core and cut into segments. Sprinkle over the lemon juice. Heat the oil and add the onion, beetroot, spices, and stock and simmer for 10 minutes. Add the apple segments and simmer, uncovered, for 2 minutes. Season with salt and pepper.

Heat some ghee. Ladle in 3 portions of the mixture and fry for 3-4 minutes until golden brown. Turn the blinis and fry the other side. Remove and keep warm. Repeat with the remaining mixture.

Heat the buckwheat in the frying pan. Place 3 blinis on each plate and top with some ragout and a spoonful of sour cream. Garnish with the dill tips and the buckwheat, and serve.

Serves 2:
100g (31/2 oz) buckwheat flour
100ml (31/2 fl oz) cold water
150ml (5fl oz) hot water
1 sachet active dried yeast
1/2 tsp honey
Salt
400g (14oz) beetroot
150g (5oz) onion
1 cooking apple
2-3 tbsp lemon juice
1 tbsp sunflower oil
Pinch of mixed spice
100ml (31/2 fl oz) vegetable stock
Pepper
2-3 tbsp ghee or clarified butter
3-4 tbsp buckwheat
2 tbsp sour cream (20% fat)
2 tbsp dill

PER PORTION: 644 kcal• 13 g protein • 30 g fat • 80 g carbohydrate

Wok-fried

quick and nourishing

Amaranth

Serves 2:
100g (3½ oz) amaranth (page 20)
1 tsp dried lemon grass
200ml (7fl oz) fermented wheat liquid (page 15)
2 spring onions
300g (10oz) young carrots
200g (7oz) mushrooms
2 tbsp corn oil
50g (scant 2oz) skinned almonds
100g (3½ oz) soy bean sprouts
1 tbsp sesame oil
Soy sauce

Bring the amaranth, lemon grass, and fermented wheat liquid to the boil. Simmer for 15 minutes. Wash and trim the spring onions and cut into thin slices. Wash and trim the carrots, then peel them and cut them into slices. Wipe the mushrooms and, depending on the size, cut them into four or eight pieces.

Heat the corn oil in a wok over a medium heat and stir-fry the almonds until they start to smell. Then add the carrots and stir-fry briefly.

Add the mushrooms, spring onions, and soy bean sprouts and stir-fry for 5 minutes. Add the amaranth and the sesame oil, stir-fry for a moment and add the soy sauce. Remove the lemon grass and serve immediately.

Gentle cooking with a wok

A wok is ideal for cooking small portions, and because the ingredients are cut into small pieces, the cooking is quick and the nutrients are retained. This recipe can also be made with cooked millet, quinoa, millet, or wholewheat pasta (non-egg) instead of amaranth. Other possible vegetables include Chinese cabbage, broccoli florets, kohlrabi, spinach, peppers and other types of bean sprouts.

PER PORTION:

613 kcal

21 g protein

41 g fat

43 g carbohydrate

Potato
with rocket and fromage frais
Gratin

Wash the potatoes and cook them in a steamer. Add the cream and the cheese to the vegetable stock and bring to the boil. Mix the cornflour in the water, add to the sauce, and stir until thick. Season well with salt and pepper. Wash the rocket and shake it dry. Cut into pieces and add to the sauce. Preheat the oven to 200°C/400°F. Grease a small flat gratin dish (capacity 1 litre/1¾ pints). Peel and slice the potatoes.

Peel and halve the apples and remove the core. Slice into segments. Arrange alternate layers of potato and apple in the gratin dish and pour over the sauce. Top with the sunflower seeds. Bake the gratin in the middle of the oven for 30 minutes until golden brown.

Serves 2:
500g (1lb 2oz) potatoes
250ml (8fl oz) vegetable stock
4 tbsp single cream
2 tbsp soft herb cheese
2 tsp cornflour
2 tbsp water
Salt
Pepper
100g (4oz) rocket
Butter for the dish
2 small cooking apples
40g (1½ oz) sunflower seeds

Herbs

Herbs are always alkaline and they are high in vitamins and minerals. Consumed in large quantities, they are highly therapeutic and can be used for medicinal purposes. Like cress, rocket contains large quantities of mustard oils, which aid the digestion and fight infections.

PER PORTION:

407 kcal

11 g protein

19 g fat

51 g carbohydrate

Courgettes on
courgettes and tomato juice – an alkaline aid
Tomato Amaranth

Place the amaranth in a saucepan with the tomato juice, a little salt, pepper, and the thyme and bring to the boil. Simmer gently over a low heat for 15 minutes. Meanwhile, wash and trim the courgettes. Using a sharp knife, cut them into fan shapes and then gently spread the segments out. Preheat the oven to 200°C/400°F. Grease a small, flat gratin dish (capacity 1 litre/1¾ pints).

Combine the amaranth with the olive oil, pour into the gratin dish, and level with a spoon. Lay the courgette "fans" on top.

Mix the hazelnuts with the Parmesan and sprinkle over the courgettes. Place the dish in the centre of the oven and bake for 20 minutes until golden brown.

Serves 2:

150g (5oz) amaranth (page 20)
300ml (10fl oz) tomato juice
Salt
White pepper
1/2 tsp thyme
500g (1lb 2oz) small courgettes (zucchini)
1-2 tbsp olive oil
3 tbsp ground hazelnuts
3 tbsp grated Parmesan
Oil for the dish

PER PORTION: 584 kcal • 22 g protein • 31 g fat • 58 g carbohydrate

Plum
with cinnamon and hazelnuts
Dumplings

Wash the potatoes and cook them in a steamer for 20-30 minutes. Peel

while still hot and push them through a potato ricer. Carefully mix with a

pinch of salt, the flour, and as much potato flour as

necessary to make the mixture malleable. Wash the

plums. Select the 12 best and dry them. Divide the

potato dough into 12 pieces, press a plum into the

centre of each piece, and gently roll into a ball.

Halve the remaining plums and remove the stones.

Poach gently with half the cinnamon and the water.

Stir 2 tbsp agave or maple syrup into the compote

and chill.

Serves 2:
500g (1lb 2oz) floury potatoes
Salt
3 tbsp flour
2-3 tbsp potato flour
400g (14 oz) plums
1 tsp cinnamon
2 tbsp water
2 tbsp butter
4 tbsp agave or maple syrup
2 tbsp grated hazelnuts

In another saucepan, bring plenty of salted water to

the boil. Place the dumplings in the water and simmer, uncovered, for 10

minutes until they rise to the top. Remove with a slotted spoon and leave

to drain.

Heat the butter in a frying pan and roast the nuts. Add the remaining

cinnamon and turn the plum dumplings in this mixture. Pour over the

remaining syrup and serve with the compote.

power

PER PORTION: 538 kcal • 8 g protein • 14 g fat• 94 g carbohydrate

Redcurrant
light and refreshing
Sorbet

Wash and sort the redcurrants, remove from the stalks and leave to drain.

Purée the berries and press through a sieve. Add the agave or maple syrup.

Serves 2:

250g (9oz) redcurrants

100ml (3 1/2 fl oz) agave or maple syrup

Pinch of cinnamon

Mineral water

Place the mixture in the freezer, stirring every 30 minutes, until frozen.

Transfer to the refrigerator about 30 minutes before serving. Add 100ml (3 1/2 fl oz) mineral water per glass to the sorbet. Stir the sorbet well, divide between two glasses.

* Fruity desserts

These dishes are alkaline-forming provided they do not contain large amounts of dairy products, egg, white flour, gelatine or sugar. Use agar agar instead of gelatine, cornflour or arrowroot instead of flour, cocoa powder instead of chocolate, and honey, maple syrup, dried fruit or syrup instead of sugar. Light agave syrup is a gastronomic novelty, relatively neutral in flavour, easy to dissolve and affordable. Maple syrup can be used in place of agave syrup.

PER PORTION:

216 kcal

1 g protein

1 g fat

51 g carbohydrate

Chocolate
sweetened with dried dates
Pudding

Serves 2: • 8 dried dates • 500ml (20fl oz) full-fat milk • 5 tbsp cocoa powder •

30g (generous 1oz) cornflour

Wash and skin the dates and remove the stones. Purée, then gradually add the milk

and cocoa powder. Bring to the boil, stirring constantly. Mix the cornflour with 2 tbsp

cold water, add to the cocoa and simmer gently for 1 minute over a low heat. Divide

between 2 dessert bowls and chill.

PER PORTION: 314 kcal • 12 g protein • 10 g fat • 43 g carbohydrate

Tropical
with lime juice and pineapple
Jelly

Serves 2: • 1 small pineapple • 3 oranges • 1 lime • 10g (1/4 oz) agar agar for setting • 2-3 tbsp honey

Peel the pineapple and cut into slices. Remove the woody core and cut the slices into pieces.

Peel and divide 2 oranges into segments, saving the juice. Squeeze the remaining orange and

the lime. Add enough water to the juice to make 250ml (8fl oz) of liquid. Remove 2-3 tbsp and

mix with the agar agar. Bring the remaining juice to the boil, stir in the agar agar, and boil for

1-2 minutes. Stir in the honey and fruit and chill for at least 4 hours.

PER PORTION: 162 kcal • 1 g protein • 1 g fat • 38 g carbohydrate

Semi-frozen Flummery

serve with berry-banana purée

Combine the yoghurt, powdered vanilla, honey, and lemon peel and stir until smooth and creamy. Add the agar agar and leave to stand for 15 minutes. Then simmer gently in a small saucepan for 2-3 minutes, and leave to cool. Add the egg yolk when the cream starts to set at the edges. Whip the cream until stiff and fold in.

Line a small mould or dish with aluminium foil (shiny side up). Grease the foil. Pour the mixture into the prepared mould and place in the freezing compartment of the refrigerator for at least 6 hours. To serve, carefully remove the flummery from the mould, discard the foil, and leave the dessert to stand for 30 minutes.

Meanwhile, squeeze the juice from the lemon. Peel and slice the banana and purée with the lemon juice and honey. Add the banana purée to the berries. Serve the flummery with the fruit purée.

Serves 2:
150ml (5fl oz) yoghurt
1/2tsp powdered vanilla
40g (1¹/2 oz) cloverleaf honey
1 tsp grated lemon peel
1 tsp agar agar
1 egg yolk
100g (3¹/2 fl oz) whipping cream
Oil for the dish
For the sauce:
1 lemon
1 banana
2-3 tbsp honey
200g (7oz) raspberries

PER PORTION: 493kcal • 7g protein • 23g fat • 67g carbohydrate

INDEX to recipes
Anti stress

Abbreviations:

tsp = teaspoon
tbsp = tablespoon

Most of the ingredients required for the recipes in this book are available from supermarkets and health food stores. For more information, contact the following importers of organic German produce:-
The Organic Food Company, Unit 2, Blacknest Industrial Estate, Blacknest Road, Alton GU34 4PX;
(T) 01420 520530 (F) 01420 23985

Windmill Organics, 66 Meadow Close, London SW20 9JD
(T) 0181 395 9749 (F) 0181 286 4732

Fermented Wheat Juice is produced in Germany by Kanne Brottrunk GMBH
(T) 00 49 2592 97400 (F) 00 49 2592 61370

Further information on German food importers is available from The Central Marketing Organisation
(T) 0181 944 0484 (F) 0181 944 0441

First published in the UK by
Gaia Books Ltd., 20 High St
Stroud, GL5 1AZ

Registered at 66 Charlotte St,
London W1P 1LR
Originally published under the title
Säure Basen Balance

© 1999 Gräfe und Unzer Verlag GmbH
Munich. English translation copyright
© 1999 Gaia Books Ltd.
Translated by Mo Croasdale in association
with First Edition Translations Ltd,
Cambridge, UK.

All rights reserved. No part of this book
may be copied in any way or broadcast on
film, radio or TV, or reproduced photo-
mechanically, on tape or using a data
processing system without the written
approval of the publisher.

Reproduction: MRM Graphics Ltd,
Winslow, UK.
Printed in Singapore by Imago

ISBN 1 85675 155 4
A catalogue record for this book is
available in the British Library

10 9 8 7 6 5 4 3 2

Caution
The techniques and recipes in this book
are to be used at the reader's sole
discretion and risk.
Always consult a doctor if you are in doubt
about a medical condition.

Dagmar Freifrau von Cramm
Studied ecotrophology, and after
graduation began to practise nutritional
theory in cooking. The mother of three
sons, she has been a freelance food
journalist since 1984. She has been a
member of the Presiding Committee of
the German Society for Nutrition since
1996.

Photos: FoodPhotography Eising, Munich

Susie M. and **Pete Eising** have studios in
Munich and Kennebunkport, Maine/USA.
They studied at the Munich Academy of
Photography, where they established their
own studio for food photography in 1991.

Food styling: **Monika Schuster**

Vitamin Diet

Lose weight naturally with fresh fruit and vegetables
Angelika Ilies
£4.99
ISBN 1 85675 145 7
All the benefits of eating fresh fruit and vegetables plus a natural way to weight loss.

Energy Drinks

Power-packed juices, mixed, shaken or stirred
Friedrich Bohlmann
£4.99
ISBN 1 85675 140 6
Fresh juices packed full of goodness for vitality and health

Detox

Foods to cleanse and purify from within
Angelika Ilies
£4.99
ISBN 1 85675 150 3
Detoxify your body as part of your daily routine by eating nutritional foods that have cleansing properties

Anti Stress

Recipes for Acid-Alkaline Balance
Dagmar von Cramm
£4.99
ISBN 1 85675 155 4
A balanced diet to reduce stress levels, maximise immunity and help you keep fit

For a catalogue of titles please call 01453 752985 or visit our website www.gaiabooks.co.uk